I0568198

FIGHTING GOD'S WAY!

Strategic Keys to Winning Battles in the Spirit!

by Pastor Tom Carubba

SHABAR PUBLICATIONS
www.shabarpublications.com

Most Shabar Publications products are available at special quantity discounts for bulk purchase for sales promotions, fund-raising and educational needs.

For details, write Shabar Publications at mayorga1126@gmail.com.

Fighting God's Way! by Pastor Tom Carubba

Published by Shabar Publications
3833 N. Taylor Rd.
Palmhurst, Texas 78573
www.shabarpublications.com

ISBN 978-1-955433-07-5

Table of Contents

Preface

We live in a fallen world! Most of society is corrupt as well. Ever since Adam and Eve rebelled and disobeyed God, there has been chaos and torment. Rebellion and disobedience set the stage for Satan to come in and take dominion over the world that was originally planned and designed for good and not evil.

Satan would have us think that he has control and that we, the church, can't stop him or do anything against him and his kingdom. My friends, the devil is dead wrong!

Jesus came to give us the power and authority to defeat Satan's tactics and devices. Jesus has given us weapons that are not carnal, but mighty through Him for the pulling down of stronghold – yes, and Satan has established many strongholds in society!

Too many Christians don't know the extent of the power and authority Jesus has restored and given to us to combat demonic forces. Many have failed to realize who we are in Jesus Christ. Many have become distracted with growing our ministries, our careers, and fulfilling our personal dreams and desires. This is happening in such a great way that we have forgotten that we are soldiers in the army of God.

The reason we have forgotten that we are in God's army is because many don't even think we are in a war. Many believers face opposition and attacks from the enemy and do nothing to fight back against those attacks. Satan is attacking us, our families the Church and our nation with fierce strategies of warfare. If we do not know how to fight back, then Satan will have his way!

Inside this manual, I have compiled truths in the Word of God that will make us effective in our battles against Satan and his kingdom. The truths contained in this manual will expose the lies we have believed from Satan. It will also help the believer uncover demonic strategies and counter it with strategies designed specifically by God, to not only confront Satan and his schemes, but to defeat him!

I believe that now is the time for the church of Jesus Christ to arise in warfare and into the next level of victory! We cannot stay hidden anymore; we can't pretend that things are fine anymore! The future of our children and grandchildren, depends on what we are willing to do for them today!

Are you ready to stop hiding in fear and to start fighting? The battle is the Lord's He has guaranteed

4

our victory. All we must do is learn about our God-given authority, learn how to use His weapons that He has provided for us – and we shall prevail in the powerful name of Jesus! Get ready to fight!

-Pastor Tom Carubba

Introduction

Let's suppose you were a captain of a large army. When recruits first came under your command, most were given an instructional manual. This manual not only instructed them on everything they needed to know about waging a successful war, but also taught them on the nature, purpose, and the strategies of the enemy.

However, what would you do as their captain, if you knew that most of the soldiers under your command were unfamiliar with their war manual and to make matters worse, they didn't even realize that there was a war going on?

What would you do if great numbers of your troops were out of uniform and poorly armed, not even knowing they had weapons, much less, how to use them? What would you do if many were sick or wounded? What would you do if you knew that some of your troops were unwillingly cooperating with the enemy? What would you do if you knew there was also a strong "fifth column" at work among your troops? What would you do if the few warriors who actually knew how to fight and make war, were frequently held in disdain by their fellow soldiers?

The above situations may sound foolish, but it is the one in which Jesus Christ, Commander in Chief of the heavenly armies finds Himself today.

Much of our Christianity today don't even realize that they are in a war, a war for their souls, a war for their families, and war for Jesus' Church. While our enemy Satan, prowls about seeking whom he may devour, much of the Christian world stands at ease, frightened, depressed or discouraged over what our enemy is doing, never realizing that it is Christians who make up the companies, squadrons, and divisions of God's army.

This manual was compiled with the vision to teach Christians their part and responsibility in this spiritual warfare. *Charles Spurgeon* said in his last sermon to the young men and women in his service, ***"that if you really understood the goodness of God, you would rush to be enlisted in His service."***

Let us be quick to learn, so that we may become a good soldier of Jesus Christ, fighting the good fight of faith and enduring hardships as a good soldier!

Chapter 1

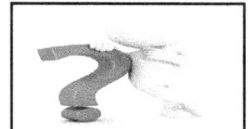

Who Am I and What Am I Doing Here?

WAR! Most of us don't even like to think about war much less participate in it. There are some who take an extreme position, claiming that if Jesus was alive today, He would be a pacifist, condemning war in all its forms. These people also reject all Old Testament idea of God as a "man of war" and interpret such Scripture as mistaken concepts of a primitive people, or as myths and allegories. They cannot visualize the Lord Himself leading an army as its Captain, sending people out to battle, setting ambushes and teaching men to fight.

It may come as a surprise to many, therefore, that much of the New Testament is written from the point of view that we are in a world which conducts business as usual against the backdrop of a fierce war raging between two kingdoms – Christ's Kingdom of light and Satan's domain, the kingdom of darkness.

Whether we will accept it or not, the Christian has a very definite role to play in this warfare. We might go so far as to say that one of our chief roles as Christians is taking our part in this warfare.

Whereas the Old Testament describes warfare in the natural realm in the New Testament we are called to wage a far different kind of warfare.

A Different Kind Of Warfare
Read 2 Corinthians 10:3-4

1. What does Paul say he does not do? _____
   _____
   _____
   _____

2. What does he say about the weapons he uses? _____
   _____
   _____

7

The translation in the NIV expresses it differently: *"The weapons we fight with are not the weapons of the world. On the contrary, they have divine power to demolish strongholds."*

In other words, Paul is saying that he is not fighting a natural but a spiritual war, and spiritual warfare uses spiritual weapons. Read 2 Timothy 2:3-4

3. What does Paul call Timothy? _____

_____

_____

_____

In reminding Timothy to be a good soldier, Paul had in mind the Roman soldier that rigorously trained and disciplined himself as a member of the Roman army which had conquered most of the known world of that day.

4. What does a good soldier do (v.4)? _____

_____

_____

_____

The Roman soldier was expected to keep one thing in mind, the service of his commander. The Roman soldier was not allowed to marry and was not permitted to become involved in any kind of business or trade apart from the army.

Group Discussion: Who is Paul referring to when he writes about the one who enlists us?

Personal Questions: Are there areas in your life in which your chief aim is not to please Jesus? If there are, what are you going to do about them?

5. What else was the soldier supposed to do (V.3)? _____

_____

_____

_____

Roman soldiers were experts at enduring hardship. Their life was very difficult, and the weapons, equipment and rations they carried were heavy. Frequently stationed thousands of miles from home in a foreign country and living among hostile people, these men served under requirements of duty that most of us cannot understand.

Personal Questions: Has serving Jesus caused you to suffer (endure) hardship? Why or why not?

Members Of An Occupational Army

The Roman soldier of Jesus' and Paul's day did not always spend his life fighting. Part of the time he served as a member of an occupational army that lived in one of the conquered countries. Not only was this army there to maintain peace, it also had to be prepared to keep the former rulers and citizens of the country from trying to regain control. Roman soldiers had still another important job. They were expected to spread the Roman culture and generally to "Romanize" the part of the world to which they were assigned. Sometimes, upon retirement, they received a grant of land and so they spent their remaining days as part of this Roman colony, a little bit of Rome, any miles from home.

When a man enlisted in the Roman army, he either automatically received Roman citizenship or it was granted to him after his term of service. No matter how long he might live apart from Rome, no Roman soldier or citizen ever gave up his Roman citizenship. Peter and Paul also saw us as citizens of another "country." Read 1 Peter 2:11.

6. What does Peter call his readers? _____

_____

_____

_____

7. Where is our citizenship? _____

_____

_____

_____

Group Discussion: How does the idea of our being a member of an occupational army change your thinking as to your role as a Christian? As part of that occupational army on earth, what should we be doing?

Take a look at two other illustrations given in the Bible which will help better explain our position as part of God's spiritual army.

Read Joshua 1:2-3

8. How did the Israelites receive the Promised Land? _____

_____

_____

Read Joshua 1:6

9. What did God promise Joshua if he would be strong and courageous?

_____

_____

_____

Although God had given the Promised Land to the Israelites, they still had to take possession of it. This taking possession of a land which had already been given to a people is a second picture of our spiritual warfare. In the beginning, God gave Adam and Eve title to the earth. Then, by their act of disobedience to the Lord, they, in fact, turned over dominion of the earth to Satan. With His death on the cross, Jesus gained back the legal ownership. However, He did not take possession of it. God has given us the job of possessing the land.

Following any war, there are often pockets of enemy resistance, rebellious troops that will not give up until forced to. There are collaborators and individuals who try to play both camps. It is our job to drive out those illegal inhabitants. We will meet resistance, for even though Satan is a defeated enemy, he is still at loose on the earth, prowling "about as a roaring lion" seeking someone to devour.

A City On A Hill

The Bible gives us another picture that we use to help us understand our role in spiritual warfare.

Ancient Israelite cities frequently had two main protective devices: First, they were built on the brow of the highest hill in the area, and second, they were protected by strong walls.

In Matthew 5:14, Jesus calls the Christian a "city on a hill."

This image can be used as an illustration of a Christian's defensive warfare. Sitting high on a hill where it can clearly be seen, the "city on the hill" also has the advantage of being able to see the approach of the enemy. The condition of the walls that surround this city may well be safe from attack or at the mercy of the enemy.

You might be wondering: Why did God entrust this important job of warfare to us when He could have done the job so much better Himself? Of course, we will never know the complete story until we reach Heaven, but the Bible has given us a few hints.

Read I Corinthians 6:2-3

10. What does Paul tell the Corinthians we wll do in the new earth?

_____

_____

_____

Read 2 Timothy 2:12

11. What is promised us in this verse? _____

_____

_____

_____

Read Revelation 5:9-10

12. What is granted to God's Kingdom of priest? _____

_____

_____

_____

The future God has planned for His people is beyond our comprehension and imagination. But one part of His plan He has revealed – we are to reign with Him. Spiritual warfare is on-the-job training for our future reigning with Christ.

TO DO:

This week try to seriously visualize yourself as a soldier in an occupational army. You are a citizen of Heaven and your Commander in Chief has sent you to the place where you presently live. See how many ways you can reflect the culture of your "native" land. Remember you are in this world to "heavenize" its culture, to maintain peace, to fight off any rebellious attacks of the defeated enemy and to keep him from resuming any kind of leadership.

At the end of the week ask yourself:
1. Was I always a good soldier?
2. Did I always try to please the one who enlisted me?
3. If the answer to either question 1 or 2 was a no, what things or conditions has caused

me the most problems?

4. What will I do differently in the future?

MEMORIZE:

"For the weapons of our warfare are not carnal but mighty in God for pulling down strongholds..." (2 Corinthians 10:4-5)

"You therefore must endure hardship as a good soldier of Jesus Christ. No one engaged in warfare entangles himself with the affairs of this life, that he may please him who enlisted him as a soldier." (2 Timothy 2:3-4)

Chapter 2

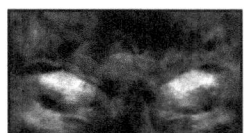

Who's The Enemy?

We covered a lot of ground in the first chapter, ground that we will be looking at much more closely in other chapters. Before we go on, we need to make sure we've retained the important principles from chapter one.

The two illustrations of offensive Christian warfare were –

_____

_____

_____

The illustration of defensive warfare was –

_____

_____

_____

Paul said the kind of warfare we are engaged in is _____ warfare.

Group Discussion: If you are in a group, share the experiences you have had during the week as a member of God's army of occupation.

Know your enemy. Whether warfare is in the natural or the spiritual, if we are to be successful in waging it, learning as much as possible about the enemy is one of the fundamental requirements.

Any information we can gain about the origin of Satan and his powers must come from the Bible. The writers of Scripture have not devoted a lot of space to informing us about the nature of our enemy, but they have given us more information than most people realize.

Read Isaiah 14:12-15 and Ezekiel 28:11-19

Most Biblical authorities agree that these two references refer to Satan and give us details of his history.

Past History

1. Who was Satan? _____
_____
_____

2. What is the description given of him? _____
_____
_____
_____

3. What are some of the titles he was called? _____
_____
_____
_____

4. What was his condition at creation? _____
_____
_____
_____

Do these passages conflict with your ideas of Satan? Have you been taken in by the comic book picture of him as a humorous little guy in red pajamas? One of Satan's most successful devices has been "passing himself off" as harmless and not too bright.

5. What caused Satan's downfall? _____
_____
_____
_____

When Satan was created by God, he was beautiful in all aspects. This beauty eventually became the source of his fall.

Read Revelation 12:7-10
6. What do these verses describe? _____
_____

7. What was the result of that war? _____
_____
_____
_____

Read Psalm 103:20
8. What do angels excel in? _____
_____
_____
_____

Both from the Bible and from experience, it seems safe to conclude that although he was banished from Heaven, Satan lost none of his powers or rank (even beauty) through his disgrace. Satan always has been and is today a formidable enemy. Many of the names used for him in Scripture reflect this idea.

Many Names And Faces

9. Beside each reference write the name given –
   Matthew 10:25 _____
   _____

   Luke 4:2 _____
   _____

   John 12:31 _____
   _____

   John 14:30 _____
   _____

   2 Corinthians 4:4 _____
   _____

   Ephesians 2:2 _____
   _____

1 Peter 5:8 _____

_____

10. The Bible also has much to say about the character of Satan. Give the characteristic that is either given or suggested in the following Scripture –

Genesis 3:1 (2 Corinthians 11:3) _____

_____

Job 1:6; Matthew 4:3-10 _____

_____

Job 1:9; Job 2:4 _____

_____

Luke 8:29; Luke 9:39 _____

_____

2 Corinthians 1:14; Ephesians 6:11 _____

_____

Ephesians 2:2; Ephesians 6:12 _____

_____

1 Timothy 3:6 _____

_____

James 4:7 _____

_____

1 John 2:13 _____

_____

Group Discussion: Are there any characteristics on this list that are new or come as a surprise to you?

Generally speaking, most people are inclined to either give Satan and his legions too much power, or be ignorant or disregard those powers. What does the Bible say those powers are?

Diversionary Tactics
Read Matthew 4:3-10

In this familiar story in Christ's life, following His 40 days in the wilderness, we find the devil trying to direct Jesus away from His main purpose by tempting Him.

Group Discussion: Can you share an experience of a time Satan tempted you? Was he successful or how did you withstand him?

Read Psalm 91:11-12
This is the Scripture to which Satan was referring.

11. What two important lines does Satan omit in the Matthew Scripture?

_____

_____

_____

From the above example we can say that Satan can misinterpret (misapply) or pervert Scripture.

Group Discussion: One of the chief devices the enemy uses today is misinterpreting or misapplying Scripture. All cults are based on doctrinal errors, the misinterpretation of Scripture.

Read Matthew 13:19
12. What does the evil one (Satan) do in this verse? _____

_____

_____

_____

Read John 13:2
13. What had Satan done to Judas Iscariot? _____

_____

_____

_____

Read Luke 13:10-16

14. With whom is this Scripture concerned? _____

_____

_____

15. Who does Jesus say caused her illness (v.16)? _____

_____

_____

_____

Of course, illness can be caused by our own living habits.

Read John 13:27

16. Previously, Satan had been content to put ideas into Judas' mind. Now he goes one step further. He _____ Judas.

Satan Powers

Read Acts 5:1-11

17. In this familiar story of Ananias and Sapphira, what dos Peter say to Ananias in verse 3? _____

_____

_____

Read Acts 10:38

18. This Scripture tells us that Satan has the power to _____ people.

Read 2 Corinthians 4:4

19. What power does Satan have over the unbelievers according to this verse?

_____

_____

_____

Have you ever wondered how people can remain oblivious to the Lord and what He is doing in the earth today? This, of course, is the answer. Today, as in Paul's day, Satan continues to blind the mind of the unbelieving, keep them from seeing the glory of Christ.

Read 2 Corinthians 11:4

20. Paul says that Satan has the power _____

_____

_____

_____

Group Discussion: Have you ever had the experience of Satan appearing to you as an angel of light?

Read 1 Thessalonians 2:18

21. What has Satan been guilty of in this verse? _____

_____

_____

_____

Read I Timothy 3:7

22. Paul warns believers not to become involved in slander and incur reproach. Why?

_____

_____

_____

Read Hebrews 2:14 and Revelation 1:18

23. Finally, Satan has the power of _____

_____

_____

_____

24. However, what did Christ do to Satan? _____

_____

_____

_____

25. Who holds the keys to life and death? _____

_____

_____

_____

No Christian needs to ever be afraid to die. Although death is still operative today, and is the final enemy abolished by Christ, only our physical body dies. Life here is merely one stage of our eternal life in the Lord. When we are released from our physical body, our spirit then will go to be with Christ.

26. Summarize what you have learned about Satan's powers. _____

_____

_____

_____

_____

_____

Satan Is Not Alone

Now that we have taken a look at Satan, we need to realize that he does not stand alone. He is commander in chief of a vast malignant horde, ready to do his bidding.

Although the Bible does not specifically give us the makeup of this army, careful study can tell us much about the powers of these troops.

Reread Revelations 12:7-9

27. What is happening in these verses? _____

_____

_____

_____

28. Who are the adversaries? _____

_____

_____

_____

29. What was the result of this war? _____

_____

_____

_____

If we can interpret these verses to be a picture of what happen in heaven when Satan rebelled, then we can see that at that time many of the angels of heaven sided with him and will someday share his doom. Some commentators believe that the stars in

Revelation 12:4 refer to angels. If this is true, a full one-third of all the heavenly host rebelled with Satan.

Read Ephesians 6:12

30. What are the four descriptions of Satan's forces given in this verse?

_____

_____

_____

_____

_____

Enemy Strategy
Read I Samuel 16:14

31. We find an evil spirit _____ Saul.

Read 1 Kings 22:22

32. What kind of an evil spirit is named in this verse? _____

Read Matthew 8:28-32

33. What was wrong with the two men Jesus encountered? _____

_____

_____

_____

34. What characterized their possession? _____

_____

_____

_____

35. What did the demons say to Jesus? _____

_____

_____

_____

36. What did Jesus do? _____

_____

_____

_____

These verses give us a significant amount of information concerning demons. They can possess people, they can cause them to be violent, they recognize who Jesus is even when men do not, and they are subject to Jesus.

Read Luke 11:14

37. What did demon possession do to the man in these verses?

_____

_____

_____

Read Matthew 12:22

38. What was the result of the demon possession in the case of this man?

_____

_____

_____

Read Matthew 17:14-16

39. How did demon possession affect the son of this man? _____

_____

_____

_____

Read Acts 16:16-18

40. What kind of an evil spirit did the slave girl have? _____

_____

_____

_____

41. What did the spirit enable her to besides fortune telling? _____

_____

_____

_____

Read 2 Corinthians 12:7

42. What power of Satan does Paul reveal here? _____

_____

_____

_____

Read 1 Timothy 4:1-3

43. What does Paul say will happen in "latter times?" _____

_____

_____

_____

Read Daniel 10:12-13

44. Daniel had been praying for twenty-one days. What reason did Gabriel give for the delay in the answer? _____

_____

_____

_____

_____

This verse shows us that there are powerful demons in control of counties. So powerful was this "prince of the kingdom of Persia" that he withstood the archangel Gabriel.

Consorting With The Enemy

How does anyone come under Satan's influence and finally his power? The Bible tells us God's position on our having to do with satanic activity very clearly.

Read Deuteronomy 18:9-11

45. What is forbidden in this verse? _____

_____

_____

_____

46. List the forbidden practices given here. _____

_____

_____

_____

Some modern day variations of these forbidden practices are fortunetelling horoscopes, ouija boards, mind expanding drugs, séances, clairvoyance, and all other involvement with the occult.

Personal Question: Have you ever been guilty of any of these practices? If you have, you must renounce them and ask the Lord's forgiveness.

We, as Christians, do not have to fear Satan, even though he at times seems formidable. We have a mighty, all knowing, all powerful conquering Commander in Chief, Jesus Christ.

TO DO:

At home this week go over the lists of Satan's characteristics and powers. Can you see ways he has influence, hindered or affected you? What are you going to do about them? What will you do to keep the same things from happening again? (Be careful not to blame Satan for problems of your own making)

MEMORIZE:

"**For we do not wrestle against flesh and blood, but against principalities, against powers, against the rulers of the darkness of this age, against spiritual hosts of wickedness in the heavenly places.**" (Ephesians 6:12)

"**Little children, let no one deceive you. He who practices righteousness is righteous, just as He is righteous. He who sins is of the devil, for the devil has sinned from the beginning. For this purpose the Son of God was manifested, that He might destroy the works of the devil.**" (I John 3:7-8)

Chapter 3

Our Commander In Chief

In the last chapter we took a look at the commander in chief of the enemy forces. Now we want to turn our eyes to a very different picture.

One of the problems God has in communicating with His people is the inability of our finite (limited) minds to grasp infinite ideas. Just as explanations to our children must be expressed in terms they can understand so God chooses examples that will help us to understand. However, earthy examples can never adequately express heavenly realities. We must always remember whenever we see a picture illustrating some spiritual principle or idea that it is, at best, a "shadow" of the substance.

War In Heaven

Let's take a look at some scenes that have happened and will happen in heaven.

First, we're going to look at a description of an event that happened in the past before the creation of earth as we know it now.

Read Revelations 12:7-9
1. What is pictured here? _____

_____

_____

_____

2. Who is fighting? _____

_____

_____

_____

3. What is the end result of this war? _____

25

_____

_____

_____

Read Daniel 10:1-13

4. When does the archangel Gabriel say Daniel's request was heard?

_____

_____

_____

5. Why was the answer delayed so long? _____

_____

_____

_____

We remember from the past chapter that this "prince" is a very important demon in Satan's hierarchy.

6. How did Gabriel finally get through? _____

_____

_____

_____

Verse 13, as translated in the Amplified Bible gives us a little more insight on Michael, "Michael, one of the chief of the celestial princes came to help me; and I remained (was not needed) there with the kings of Persia."

Among scholars who have made a study of angels, many believe that while Gabriel is a messenger angel, Michael is the head warrior angel of God's mighty army.

Command Headquarters

Read Revelation 19:11 and 14-18

7. How is the Lord described in these verses? _____

_____

_____

_____

8. Who is with Him? _____

9. What is Jesus about to do? _____

_____

_____

This scene is a picture of an event which will take place in the future of the world. It is a description of our Lord Jess Christ as Commander in Chief of the heavenly armies, as He prepares for the final battle against the forces of Satan.

It is believed that the archangel Michael is the other main participant in this drama.

A War Camp

The purpose of having you look at these scenes is to create a picture for you. We have many different pictures of the spiritual realm in the Bible, but for the purposes of this study right now, we would like you to envision it as a war camp. Commander in Chief of the heavenly forces is Jesus Christ. Under His immediate command, we see His commanding general, the archangel Michael, and under Michael are legions of warring spiritual beings making up the heavenly armies who war against the dark satanic forces.

Group Discussion: Have you ever considered heaven in this way before? Do all these warfare images disturb you? If so, why?

Read John 1:1-3
10. What do these verses tell us about the Word (Jesus)?

   a. _____
   b. _____
   c. _____

Read Hebrews 1:2-3
11. What additional facts do we learn about Jesus Christ in these verses?

_____

_____

_____

Read Hebrews 1:10

12. What does this verse tell us Christ did? _____

_____

_____

_____

_____

Read Colossians 1:16

13. What do we learn about Christ here? _____

_____

_____

_____

14. Write a summary of who Christ was before His time on earth.

_____

_____

_____

_____

_____

_____

In the above verses we can see a picture of the second Person of the Godhead, Jesus Christ, the Creator God who created the world and everything in it.

God's purposes are eternal. From the beginning it was His desire to create a race of men who would not only worship Him and have fellowship with Him, but have dominion over the earth.

Though He knew His creation would fall on its own, He had a plan from the beginning - the sending of a Savior to earth; His Name was Jesus Christ. When Jesus died on the cross, His death accomplished many things. Although we will have to wait until heaven to learn the full story, the Bible tells us much.

Front Line Duty

15. Read the following Scriptures and list the things Jesus' death accomplished.

Colossians 1:12-17 _____

_____

_____

_____

Colossians 1:18-20: _____

_____

_____

_____

2 Timothy 1:10: _____

_____

_____

_____

Hebrews 2:15: _____

_____

_____

_____

Hebrews 2:17: _____

_____

_____

_____

Hebrews 10:10: _____

_____

_____

_____

Revelation 1:5: _____

_____

_____

_____

Group Discussion: Which of these accomplishments have you been most conscious of in your life?

The implications of what Jesus did for us should stagger our minds and bring us to our knees in gratitude. But this is only part of the story. By His sacrifice, Jesus also accomplished many things against Satan.

16. Read the following Scriptures and list what was accomplished in each case.

Hebrews 2:14: _____

_____

_____

_____

1 Peter 3:19: _____

_____

_____

_____

1 John 3:8: _____

_____

_____

_____

Colossians 2:12-15: _____

_____

_____

_____

Triumphal Procession

Have you ever puzzled over what Colossians 2:12-15 was actually talking about? The Colossians reference has in mind the Roman military triumphal procession, "granted to conquerors only when certain conditions had been fully complied with."

Among these, it was required that the victory be complete and decisive; that it should be over a foreign foe; that at least five thousand of the enemy should be slain in a single battle; that the conquest should extend the territory of the state, and put an end to war. When the day arrived, the people crowded the streets and filled every place from which a good view of the procession could be seen.

The temples were all open and decorated with flowers, while incense smoked from every altar. Fragrant odors from burning spices were profusely scattered through the temples and along the streets, loading the air with their perfume. In the procession were the senate and chief citizens of the state, who by their presence honored the conqueror. The richest spoils of war, such as gold, silver, weapons of every description, rare and costly works of art, and everything that was deemed most valuable by either conqueror or vanquished, were carried in open view of the crowded city. The prisoners of war were also compelled to march in the procession. The general, in whose honor the triumph was decreed, rode in a chariot drawn by four horses. His robe was embroidered with gold, and his tunic with flowers. In his right hand was a laurel bough, and in his left hand a scepter (symbols of martial victory): while on his forehead there was a wreath of Delphic laurel. Amid the shouts of the soldiers and the applause of the populace, the conqueror was carried through the streets to the temple of Jupiter, where sacrifices were offered, after which there was a public feast in the temple.

- (Manners and Customs of the Bible y James Freeman; Logos, Publishers)

Group Discussion: When Christ triumphed over Satan, did He meet all the requirements given for the Roman triumphal procession? Why or why not?

The Victor

Christ's triumph over Satan and His resurrection were followed by His ascension to Heaven.

Read Ephesians 1:20-23

17. Where is Jesus today? _____

_____

_____

18. What is His position? _____

_____

_____

19. What has the Father done for Him? _____

_____

_____

Read Hebrews 1:13

20. How long will Jesus sit there? _____

_____

_____

_____

Read Philippians 2:9

21. What does the Scripture tell us about Christ's position? _____

_____

_____

_____

Read Hebrews 1:3-4

22. How does Christ stand positionally in regard to angels? _____

_____

_____

Read Psalm 102:25-27

23. What does this tell us about Christ? _____

_____

_____

_____

24. Write a paragraph describing Christ as He is today and as Commander of the heavenly armies.

_____

_____

_____

The whole world will one day pay honor to our glorious Savior and King.

TO DO:

During this next week, spend at least 15 minutes a day meditating on one of the following ideas:

1. Jesus as Commander of the heavenly armies
2. Jesus seated at the right hand of God
3. Jesus as our Intercessor

MEMORIZE:

"For by Him all things were created that are in heaven and that are on earth, visible and invisible, whether thrones or dominions or principalities or powers. All things were created through Him and for Him." (Colossians 1:16)

"You, Lord, in the beginning laid the foundation of the earth, And the heavens are the work of Your hands. They will perish, but You remain; And they will all grow old like a garment; Like a cloak You will fold them up, And they will be changed. But You are the same, And Your years will not fail." (Hebrews 1:10-12)

Lesson 4

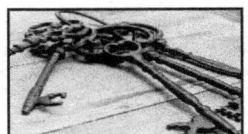

Our Authority In Christ

In the last chapter we established the position of Christ today. We know that He is seated at the right hand of God, He bears a name above even that of the angels and He is above all principalities, powers and satanic forces.

Military History

Let's begin by looking at some of the prophecy about Jesus, spoken by men inspired by the Spirit of God long before Jesus' birth in Bethlehem. Many prophets, including Isaiah spoke of a time when the Messiah would come and perform wonderful miracles on earth.

Read Isaiah 61:1-3
1. Summarize the activities of the Messiah from these verses.

_____

_____

_____

_____

Read Isaiah 11:1-2
2. What does this verse tell us? _____

_____

_____

_____

Read Isaiah 42:6-7
3. What miracles would the Messiah accomplish according to these verses?

_____

_____

_____

Read Isaiah 9:4

4. What does this verse prophesy about the Messiah? _____

_____

_____

_____

Read Isaiah 49:24-25

5. What do these verses say He will do? _____

_____

_____

_____

The religious leaders of Jesus' time were very familiar with the prophecies of Isaiah, but they were looking for a great political figure who would come as a military commander and free them from the yoke of Rome.

Consequently, when Jesus came, speaking of the establishment of a spiritual kingdom and the breaking of spiritual bonds, for the most part, they did not recognize Him as the Messiah.

Read Luke 4:18, 21, 28-29

6. Shortly after Jesus' victory over Satan in the wilderness, He returned to Nazareth, His home town. What Scripture did He read in the synagogue? _____

_____

_____

_____

7. By His reading of the Scripture from Isaiah and His statement, Jesus announced that He was the long awaited Messiah.

8. What was the reaction of those who heard Him? _____

_____

_____

The people of Jesus' time wanted a Savior who would save them from the yoke and rod of a foreign government, while Jesus wanted to rescue them from Satan.

Read Matthew 1:22-29

9. What was Jesus' response when, following the healing of the demon-possessed man, Pharisees said His power came from Satan? _____

_____

_____

_____

10. What did He say in relation to the "strong man?" _____

_____

_____

_____

_____

Group Discussion: What was Jesus saying about Himself with this illustration?

Jesus was indicating His authority over Satan. Throughout His earthly existence, Jesus showed His authority and power over the enemy and his power.

Armed Struggle

11. Read the following selections from the Gospel of Matthew and beside each reference write down the miracles Jesus performed.

Matthew 8:1-3 _____

_____

Matthew 8:28-31 _____

_____

Matthew 9:1-7 _____

_____

Matthew 9:18, 23-26 _____

_____

Matthew 9:27-30 _____

_____

Matthew 9:35 _____

_____

Matthew 14:21 _____

_____

Matthew 14:34-36 _____

_____

Matthew 15:29-31 _____

_____

Matthew 17:14-18 _____

_____

Matthew 21:18-20 _____

_____

Jesus clearly illustrated by His miracles that he indeed had authority over the works of Satan. There was still another dimension to that authority. Let's look now at the one other person who understood it well.

Delegated Authority
Read Luke 7:2-10

A centurion, a Roman officer, sent Jewish friends to Jesus asking Him to heal his highly re-garded slave who was very sick. When Jesus expressed His willingness to go to his house, the centurion told Him not to come.

12. What was his reasoning (v.8)? _____

_____

_____

_____

Group Discussion: How do we know his reasoning was correct?

No wonder Jesus was amazed at the centurion. None of His Jewish followers had truly grasped this idea. Yet here was a heathen soldier, who, understanding the nature of earthly authority, realized that heavenly authority would work in the same manner.

37

Read Matthew 10:7-8

13. On several different occasions, Jesus delegated His authority to His disciples. What instructions did He give them? _____

_____

_____

_____

_____

_____

_____

_____

Read Luke 10:8-9

14. What instructions did Jesus give the seventy? _____

_____

_____

_____

Read Mark 6:7-12

15. What did the disciples do? _____

_____

_____

_____

Read Luke 10:17

16. What was the response of the seventy when they returned? _____

_____

_____

_____

Read Matthew 28:18-20

17. After His resurrection, Jesus appeared to the eleven disciples. What did He tell them about Himself? _____

_____

_____

_____

The Commission

18. He also gave them a commission. What was that commission? _____

_____

_____

_____

_____

Read Mark 16:17-18

19. What additional information is given in these verses?

_____

_____

_____

_____

Read John 14:12

20. What had Jesus previously told the disciples on the night before He died?

_____

_____

_____

_____

Read Ephesians 1:20-23

21. After Jesus ascended into heaven, what authority was given Him?

_____

_____

_____

_____

Read Acts 1:4-8

22. Why didn't the disciples go out immediately and use the authority they had been given?_____

_____

_____

_____

23. What was it that the Father had promised? _____

_____

24. When would they receive it? _____

_____

_____

_____

Read Acts 2:1-4

25. When did this event take place? _____

_____

_____

_____

26. Write a short summary of what happen? _____

_____

_____

_____

_____

_____

_____

_____

Read Acts 2:5-12

27. What happened next? _____

_____

_____

_____

Peter, speaking the crowd, explained what had happen. Then he preached a powerful sermon, convicting them of their sin of not accepting Jesus as the long awaited Messiah.

Read Acts 2:41

28. What was the result of His message? _____

_____

_____

Power / Authority

We need to make a distinction here between power and authority. Jesus had both power and authority. That which He delegates to us is the authority to call for power. Let us give a very simple example – the policeman who directs traffic by using his hands is using authority rather than power. Obviously he does not have the power to physically stop a car whose driver decides to disregard him. However, if there is resistance to his authority, he can call for the power that stands behind his authority – more policemen, car, weapons, etc. If the driver still will not be obedient, then power may be used to stop him.

In the case of a person in charge of a company or even heading a nation, he can delegate his authority to anyone he chooses, even if that person is considered insignificant; then that person will be able to move in that authority. Should someone not respect that authority, then the representative will have at his call the power that stands behind the original authority.

Read Ephesians 2:5-6
29. What is the spiritual position of those who are in Christ? _____

_____

_____

_____

Group Discussion: We know Jesus has been given authority over all in heaven and on earth and that He is the head of the Church. We also know that the Church is the Body of Christ. Does the Body have the same authority as the head?

Group Discussion: Why do you think so few people are experiencing this truth?

One of the secrets of having the authority of God is obedience. We have Christ's authority to use in ways He would use it, not according to our own ideas or whims. The representative of any ruler must know his king's will, what the king thinks, what he wants to accomplish and how he would act if he were personally handling the situation.

TO DO:

Paul said he was an ambassador for Christ. This next week think of yourself as Christ's

41

ambassador, because that's who you are. This is a very important commission. What are your duties? Does considering yourself an ambassador require any change in your lifestyle, thinking or your daily life?

MEMORIZE:

"Most assuredly, I say to you, he who believes in Me, the works that I do he will do also; and greater works than these he will do, because I go to My Father." (John 14:12)

"The Spirit of the Lord God is upon Me, Because the Lord has anointed Me To preach good tidings to the poor; He has sent Me to heal the brokenhearted, To proclaim liberty to the captives, And the opening of the prison to those who are bound..." (Isaiah 61:1)

Chapter 5

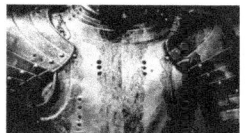

Our Armor

No commander in chief would send his army into battle without equipping it as fully as possible with all the necessary weapons. Jesus is no different and the Christian who launches into battle unarmed is foolish indeed and frequently must pay the price for their foolishness.

Let's refresh our mind by looking at a passage of Scripture which is very familiar to the heart of every Christian warrior.

Read Ephesians 6:10-18

1. Whose strength do we rely on? _____

_____

_____

_____

Group Discussion: What do you think relying on the Lord's strength means?

Relying on the Lord's strength means we are conscious that we have no power on our own apart from Him. We must never give Satan a foothold by our pride over the fact that we may become a successful warrior for the Lord. Anything we accomplish is only God's accomplishing it through us.

The Whole Armor

2. How much armor are we to take up? _____

_____

_____

_____

Most of us are wearing some or most of the armor much of the time. However, our war manual, the Bible tells us that we must take up all our armor.

3. For what purpose? _____

_____

Fighting and running are not part of the Christian's military strategy. We are to stand unwaveringly in the face of the enemy. One possible meaning for the word stand is abide.

Group Discussion: What does abiding have to do with warfare?

4. Who is our struggle against? _____

_____

_____

_____

5. What two words or phrases are repeated in verses 11 and 13? _____

_____

_____

_____

6. List the Christian's armor? _____

_____

_____

_____

_____

_____

_____

The Pieces

Read I Samuel 17

This Old Testament chapter records the familiar story of David's victory over the Philistine giant Goliath.

7. What did Saul try to give David? _____

_____

_____

_____

8. Why did David refuse them? (v. 39) _____

_____

Wisely, David did not try to go into a life-and-death battle with unfamiliar armor. He had not personally tested Saul's armor, and therefore, was unfamiliar with it.

Group Discussion: How does David's attitude toward untested armor relate to our use of spiritual armor?

Too often, we as Christians wait until we are in a perilous situation before we try to make use of the spiritual armor at our disposal. We're unfamiliar with it, or because it fits us poorly, it hampers us in our warfare.

9. What weapons did David use instead? _____

_____

_____

10. Why? _____

_____

_____

David had served his "apprenticeship" for this battle by caring for his father's sheep. He knew his weapons worked because he had proved them on the lions and bears which had attacked the sheep he was caring for.

Spiritual fighting is no different from natural fighting in this one respect. We need to serve our "apprenticeship" by winning the smaller battles that we are called upon to fight in our lives, giving us the opportunity to test both our armor and weapons.

Discussion Question: Can you relate a time when God gave you "practice" in a small battle against Satan as preparation for a bigger battle to follow?

David's victory over Goliath, a type of Satan, was a foreshadowing of Jesus' victory over our arch-enemy at Calvary?

Read Romans 13:12

11. What kind of armor doe Paul refer to in his verse? _____

_____

_____

_____

12. What does he contrast this armor with? _____

_____

_____

_____

13. What are we to do with these two "Garments?" _____

_____

_____

_____

Group Discussion: How does the Christian receive righteousness? How do we put it on?

Girded With Truth

In discussing the Christian's armor, Paul had in mind the massive armor of the Roman soldier which completely covered his body.

Read Ephesians 6:14
14. In contrast to the heavy metal covering the Roman soldier's lower body, the Christian's loins are to be covered with _____

_____

_____

_____

Read John 14:6
15. What does Jesus call Himself in this verse? _____

_____

_____

_____

16. Therefore, we can say that one interpretation of the idea of "having your loins girded with truth" could be, having your loins girded with _____

_____

_____

_____

The loins speak of our Christian walk. One purpose of the "girdle" was to strengthen the loins for a strenuous activity. Another purpose was to protect such parts of the abdomen as were not already protected by other protective coverings. So truth becomes a protection from blows of the enemy. We must be certain that our individual and daily walk is girded with Jesus.

Read John 14:17

17. What is the Holy Spirit called in this verse? _____

_____

_____

_____

Read Psalm 40:11

18. What will God's truth do? _____

_____

_____

_____

The Breastplate

Read Ephesians 6:14

19. What is the next piece of armor we are to put on? _____

_____

_____

_____

Read Isaiah 59:15-17

20. Who is putting on a breastplate of righteousness in these verses? _____

_____

_____

_____

Group Discussion: What dos the breastplate cover? What does this say about the Christian?

Read Ephesians 6:15-16

21. What is the next part of our body we are to cover? _____

_____

_____

_____

Roman military sandals were made of very strong leather. To enable the soldier to have sure footing, the soles were studded with hobnails.

The Amplified Bible translates verse 15: **"And having shod your feet in preparation** (to face the enemy with firm-footed stability, the promptness and readiness produced by the good news) **of the Gospel of peace."**

22. What is the spiritual significance of putting shoes on our feet? _____

_____

_____

_____

Group Discussion: Give an example of a time when you faced the enemy with "firm-footed stability" because you wore the Gospel of peace.

Faith As A Shield

23. What is the next piece of armor given to the Christian? _____

_____

_____

_____

24. What are we able to do with our shields? _____

_____

_____

_____

The darts used in ancient warfare were hollow reeds filled with combustible material. These were set on fire and then shot from bows. They were excellent weapons against the walled cities of the time. If the attacking army could not penetrate the walls, they could shoot flaming darts over the walls, to strike the highly combustible thatched roofs of the houses within the walls. Using water against this type of fire only spread it. The large shields used by soldiers protected them personally from these "flaming missiles."

Read James 3:5-6

25. What part of our body is described as a fire?_____

_____

_____

_____

26. How is the tongue set on fire? _____

_____

_____

_____

Personal Question: Has your tongue been the source of discomfort or even the wounding of another person? Perhaps you will want to spend time later thinking about whether your tongue has helped or hindered other Christians in their walk.

Group Discussion: How can our tongue act as a flaming missile against another Christian?

How easy it is sometimes to lend our tongue to the service of the enemy. We need to always remember that James' remarks were directed to Christians.

Read Genesis 15:1: II Samuel 22:3 and Proverbs 30:5

27. Who is our shield? _____

_____

_____

_____

Read Isaiah 21:5

28. How is a shield cared for? _____

_____

_____

_____

Shields made of several thicknesses of bullhide were stretched over a frame of wood and sometimes strengthened and ornamented with metal rims and pieces of metal. Rubbing with oil prevented the leather from drying out and cracking and the metal from rusting.

In times of battle, this oiling was especially necessary and so "anointing" the shield was equivalent to preparing for war.

Group Discussion: Oil is a symbol of the Holy Spirit. How do you "oil" your shield of faith?

Salvation As A Helmet

Read Ephesians 6:17

29. What is our next piece of armor? _____

_____

_____

_____

30. Of what is the helmet composed? _____

_____

_____

_____

Group Discussion: Is Paul talking about our salvation experience here? _____

Our salvation experience may be part of what Paul is referring to, but certainly not all of it. In addition to salvation from hell, he is talking about salvation from the dominion and power of sin, Satan and the self-life.

The helmet covers the head and thus the mind. The head speaks of authority, while a covered head speaks of submission. Isn't it interesting that the same symbol, a covered head, represents both submission and protection.

Group Discussion: Why does salvation make the perfect helmet?

The Sword

31. What other piece of armor does verse 17 refer to? _____

_____

_____

_____

32. What is the sword of the Spirit? _____

Group Discussion: How has the Word of God served as a sword in your life?

Read Hebrews 4:12

33. What does this verse say about the Word of God? _____

_____

_____

_____

34. What is it able to do? _____

_____

_____

_____

What an awesome responsibility God has given to His own word.

Read Ephesians 6:18

35. What else are we supposed to do? _____

_____

_____

TO DO:

Take this time next week to inspect your armor and your weapons. Are they cleaned and in tip top working condition? In case of an enemy attack, would you be able to use them effectively? Note any in need of repair, anything missing and make a full report on them to your Commanding Officer.

MEMORIZE:

"Finally, my brethren, be strong in the Lord and in the power of His might. Put on the whole armor of God, that you may be able to stand against the wiles of the devil." (Ephesians 6:10-11)

"The night is far spent, the day is at hand. Therefore let us cast off the works of darkness, and let us put on the armor of light." (Romans 13:12)

Chapter 6

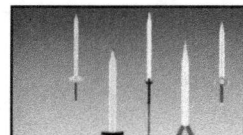

More Weapons For Our Arsenal

A major problem with the Lord's army is the fact that so many of His troops are amateurs when it comes to using the weapons at their disposal. A Christian who makes use of the many spiritual weapons available to them is the best equipped soldier in the world.

In the last chapter we looked at the armor and some of the weapons God has provided for His warriors. This chapter we're going to discover many more weapons available to us.

Enemy Sighted

Let's look at an Old Testament story that will show us how the Israelites once used God's spiritual weapons to win a tremendous victory.

Read 2 Chronicles 20:1-3
1. What was the problem facing King Jehoshaphat? _____

_____

_____

_____

2. How were they described? _____

_____

_____

_____

3. What was Jehoshaphat's firs reaction? His second? _____

_____

_____

_____

The un-renewed mind is part of our old nature. When we are attacked, it is "natural" to be afraid. The important thing is what we do in the midst of that fear.

King Jehoshaphat used one of the most important principles of spiritual warfare that we can learn. He turned his attention to seeking God. How natural it is in times of trouble to keep our attention on the problem. How natural and how wrong? By turning his attention to the Lord, King Jehoshaphat took the first step toward changing his attitude from one of defeat to one of victory.

The Christian warrior must keep their eyes on their Commander in Chief for His instructions, backed by a knowledge of both God's power and our spiritual authority in Christ.

A Different Kind Of Weapon

4. What did King Jehoshaphat do next? _____

_____

_____

_____

We cannot hope to do justice to the subject of fasting in this workbook, but it is one of the most powerful weapons in our arsenal. Fasting was an important part of the religious observance of the Jews. In Jesus' time, religious Jews fasted at least two days a week, but the practice predated Jesus by several thousand years. Although they fasted on many occasions, the Jews fasted primarily for four reasons.

Read I Samuel 7:1-6

5. Why did the people fast in this situation? _____

_____

_____

_____

Because of their recurring sin, the Israelites were defeated by the Philistines, who captured the ark of God. However, misfortune fell on the Philistines as long as they were in possession of the ark, so in time, they returned it to the Israelites.

Through the prophet Samuel God told the Israelites He would deliver them if they would remove their foreign idols and return to Him. The fasting was an act of sorrow over their sin.

Read Nehemiah 1:1-6

6. Why did Nehemiah fast? _____

_____

_____

_____

Nehemiah was the Jewish cupbearer to King Artaxerxes. Following his hearing of the pitiful conditions of the Jews in Jerusalem, he "**sat down and wept and mourned for days and ... was fasting and paying before God.**"

Read I Kings 21:20-29

7. Why did King Ahab fast? _____

_____

_____

King Ahab was one of the wicked kings in all of Israel's history. However following an encounter with the prophet Elijah, he humbled himself before the Lord with sackcloth and ashes.

Read Acts 13:2

8. What was the result of these early Christians ministering to the Lord and fasting?

_____

_____

_____

9. Considering what we have read so far, what are the primary reasons for fasting?

_____

_____

_____

Group Discussion: What do you think is accomplished when we fast?

In fasting, the human part of us is humbled and the spiritual senses are heightened, so that we are able to get ourselves out of the way and hear what God has to say to us.

Group Discussion: Can you share any experience of what God has done as you have fasted?

More Weapons

Read 2 Chronicles 20:4-13

10. Why did all the people gather together? _____

_____

_____

11. What is the essence of Jehoshaphat's prayer? _____

_____

_____

_____

As Christians we certainly do not have to remind God that we belong to Him, but we do need to turn to God in our times of trouble and warfare, keeping our eyes on Him, acknowledging and realizing that many times we are helpless to do anything about a given situation.

Read 2 Chronicles 20:14-17

12. What happen following Jehoshaphat's prayer? _____

_____

_____

_____

13. Summarize the message: _____

_____

_____

_____

_____

_____

_____

Through a prophetic message the Lord reassured King Jehoshaphat and his people that He would intervene in their behalf. Can you imagine the great joy on the part of the people at this joyous news? Prophecy, one of the gifts of the Holy Spirit available to all Christians, is frequently used at times of great urgency for reassurance and encouragement.

Group Discussion: Suppose you had been there with King Jehoshaphat and his people. Would you have had enough faith to give the word of encouragement Jahaziel gave for the Lord? Would you if you knew that the fate of a false prophet was stoning? If you had been one of the multitude that day, would you have had the faith to believe the message?

Read 2 Chronicles 20:18-19

14. What was the result of the prophetic message? _____

_____

_____

_____

There isn't enough space in all the entire world to write of the things that are accomplished in both heaven and earth when we fall down and worship the Lord. God is altogether lovely, holy and completely worthy of our worship. Somehow, when we worship God our problem is minimized and He is magnified. We, then, are willing to surrender our problem to our worthy God and He can get us out of the way long enough to deal with the problem.

The Power Of Praise

15. What else happen? _____

_____

The exhortation to praise the Lord is given more than any other in the Bible. Praise is one important weapon in our spiritual arsenal. There are many different ways to praise the Lord.

16. List the varieties of praise mentioned in the following Scriptures –

Leviticus 8:27 _____

_____

Nehemiah 8:6 _____

_____

2 Samuel 6:14 _____

_____

Psalm 33:2 _____

_____

Psalm 35:27 _____

_____

Psalm 47:1 _____

_____

Psalm 47:6 _____

_____

Psalm 95:6 _____

_____

Psalm 126:2 _____

_____

Psalm 150 _____

_____

Isaiah 12:6 _____

_____

Luke 6:23 _____

_____

Acts 10:46 _____

_____

Personal Question: How many of these ways have you praised the Lord?

Looking back over these different ways of praising God, notice how many of them are done out loud. There are times when God wants us to come before Him silently and there are many other times when He wants us to come to Him enthusiastically.

Read 2 Chronicles 20:20-21
17. What did Jehoshaphat say to his people the next morning? _____

_____

_____

18. What did he do? _____

_____

_____

_____

19. What as their position? _____

_____

_____

_____

Group Discussion: How would you like to have been a singer for King Jehoshaphat?

It would take an act of real courage to be a singer in Jehoshaphat's time – going out before the army, facing an enemy that outnumbered you tremendously. Spiritual warfare is not for the faint-hearted. Looking at this idea spiritually, we can see that singing and praising frequently go before warfare.

The Victory

Read 2 Chronicles 20:22-25
20. What happen while the people were praising and singing? _____

_____

_____

_____

21. What did the people do for the next three days? _____

_____

_____

_____

Read 2 Chronicles 20:26
22. What did they do the fourth day? _____

_____

_____

_____

The meaning of Beracah is blessing. Great was the thanksgiving to God for what He had done.

Read 32 Chronicles 20: 27-3

23 How did they return to Jerusalem? _____

_____

_____

24. What was the eventual outcome of the victory? _____

_____

_____

God has given the Christian soldier an essential part in His plan for mankind and for the world. He also given us the armor and the weapons, with which to wage crucial warfare. His training manual, the Bible, provides us with important information on how battle have been won in the past and what God's future plans are.

Group Discussion: How has the baptism in the Holy Spirit made you a better soldier?

Many people who have not received the baptism in the Holy Spirit do not recognize the nature of the spiritual warfare in which we are engaged. If you have not received the baptism in the Holy Spirit, we urge you to receive it before you attempt to become involved in spiritual conflict with the enemy.

The gifts of the Holy Spirit – tongues, interpretation cf tongues, prophecy word of wisdom, word of knowledge, discerning of spirits, the gift of healings and the working of miracles – these are the all-important weapons God has given us in our fight to occupy the world Jesus gained for us through His death on the cross and His resurrection.

TO DO:

Make sure that all of the weapons studied are in your arsenal.

MEMORIZE:

"Now when they began to sing and to praise, the Lord set ambushes against the people of Ammon, Moab, and Mount Seir, who had come against Judah; and they were defeated." (2 Chronicles 20:21)

"Let them shout for joy and be glad, Who favor my righteous cause; And let them

say continually, "Let the Lord be magnified, Who has pleasure in the prosperity of His servant." And my tongue shall speak of Your righteousness and of Your praise all the day long."(Psalm 35:27, 28)

Chapter 7

Strategy for Warfare

In the last chapter we discussed some of the problems our Commander in Chief faces – His army on earth is largely made up of volunteers and for the most part they are untrained. Many of them are scarcely aware of the warfare that rages around them. In his chapter we're going to learn some important principles about the nature of this warfare.

Principle # 1

Read Ephesians 6:12

1. Where does spiritual warfare actually take place? _____

_____

_____

2. What does this verse say our struggle is not against? _____

_____

_____

3. What is our struggle against? _____

_____

_____

_____

_____

Group Discussion: Can you think of a battle going on in your life right now that you have been attempting to fight on a human level? Does he idea that this could be a spiritual battle open up any new possibilities for handling it?

Read Daniel 10:12-14

We have already looked at this passage in chapter three, but let's review what happened. We

61

remember that the prophet Daniel was one of the Israelites who rose to an important position in the heathen empire Babylon during the dispersion of the Jews. After a frightening vision of the future, Daniel began to mourn, to fast and to pray. For twenty-one days nothing happened, but then an angelic being appeared.

4. When did the angelic being say Daniel's prayers had been heard?

_____

_____

_____

_____

5. Why hadn't the angelic being come then? _____

_____

_____

_____

6. What had finally enabled him to come? _____

_____

_____

_____

_____

In these two verses, we are given a glimpse of what is going on "behind the scenes."

Daniel had been praying and fasting for three weeks. The angelic being ad tried to come immediately in answer to his prayers, but a mighty demonic force, called here the prince of the kingdom of Persia had stopped him and held him back from completing his mission.

Finally, the archangel Michael, second in command of the heavenly armies under Jesus, came and did battle for him, allowing him to get through to Daniel.

We have only a hazy picture of what goes on in the heavenlies. We know that Babylon was a heathen country, described by some as the most idolatrous nation of all time.

Apparently, mighty forces of evil are encamped over such places, making it difficult for the righteous forces to get through.

Principle # 2

Does this say that we on earth are powerless in the face of such forces? Not at all. Remember that all the time the angelic being was struggling in the heavenlies, Daniel on earth was praying, fasting and humbling himself. Although the battle is actually fought in the heavenlies, what we do on earth has powerful influence.

Group Discussion: What is the different between Daniel and the Christian?

We must never forget that the Christian has one additional powerful weapon that was not available to Daniel. We have the authority of Jesus Christ, with which we can speak God's Word against Satan. We can bind his forces in a way that Daniel could not.

In another scene from the Old Testament, we are given a quick glimpse of God's spiritual army.

Read 2 Kings 6:15-17
7. At a bad time in the prophet's Elisha's life, his servant excitedly called his attention to what? _____
_____
_____

8. What was Elisha's answer to his fearful servant? _____
_____
_____
_____

9. Following Elisha's prayer, what did the servant see? _____
_____
_____
_____

For a brief moment, Elisha's servant was able to see what his master had already known in the Spirit that they need not fear any enemy because God's forces were surrounding them – forces which were fare greater than any earthy army. What a wonderful picture for us to keep as we face problems that seem insurmountable and battles for which victory seems an impossibility – those who are with us are more than those who are with them.

Principle # 3

Many of the intricacies of spiritual warfare may never make sense to our natural minds. God has made it very clear that His ways are not our ways (Isaiah 55:9) and that the *"foolishness of God is wiser than men."* (I Corinthians 1:24)

However, if we want to be victorious in our spiritual warfare, we must be prepared to do whatever God asks us to do, trusting that our obedience somehow influences the outcome of the actual battle raging in the heavenlies.

Read Exodus 17:8-13

10. What is the situation described here? _____

_____

_____

11. What did Moses say he would do and what did he tell Joshua to do?

_____

_____

12. What happened during the course of the battle? _____

_____

_____

13. What did Aaron and Hur do? _____

_____

_____

14. What was the result? _____

_____

_____

We have the recounting of a somewhat similar episode in the life of Joshua after he had succeed Moses as leader of the Children of Israel.

Read Joshua 8:18

15. What does the Lord tell Joshua to do? _____

_____

_____

_____

Read Joshua 8:24-26

16. What was the final result of that day? _____

_____

_____

_____

17. Why was Israel victorious? _____

_____

_____

_____

A casual reading of these two episodes gives us a curious story. We see two earthly armies locked in combat. However, the course of the battle is determined largely by what two men do – holding up a rod in the case of Moses, and stretching out a javelin toward the city to be taken in Joshua's case. What can such actions possibly have to do with the winning of two battles? We have to admit we don't know, but the two battles cannot be disputed.

We may never know exactly what happens during spiritual warfare this side of heaven, but the implication is certain – what we see is only a small part of what is actually going on, and obedience to seemingly "foolish" commands can play an important role in our warfare.

Could ever a people be given a more "foolish" set of instructions than those given to the Israelites in the taking of Jericho?

18. What did the Lord promise Joshua? _____

_____

_____

_____

19. What were His instructions? _____

_____

_____

_____

20. What did the Lord promise if the Israelites followed these instructions?

_____

_____

_____

We are familiar with this well-known story (if not, read all of Joshua 6). Joshua and the Israelites obediently followed the Lord's instructions and the walls of Jericho did fall down and the city fell into the hands of the Israelites.

Someone has humorously suggested that the reason the Lord commanded the Israelites to be silent as they marched around Jericho was to keep them from discussion their fears.

Group Discussion: How do you think you would have felt if you had been one of the soldiers marching around Jericho?

Sometimes in reading of these spectacular victories performed by the Lord for His people, we tend to think of the people involved as wholeheartedly submitting to the Lord with little anxiety. We need to remember that these were human beings with the same frailties and anxieties we have. Submitting to instructions that do not make sense to the human mind was just as difficult for them as it would be for us.

Discussion Question: Have you ever been "led" to perform some act which seemed foolish to you or went against your natural instincts, yet which resulted in spiritual victory for you?

Principle # 4

Read 2 Chronicles 20:15
21. What was the essence of the message from the Lord? _____

_____

_____

_____

_____

The battle is the Lord's. Time and time again in our spiritual warfare we will come up against this truth. While what we do on earth influences the outcome of the spiritual battle, the battle is the Lord's.

Gideon was perhaps the most reluctant "hero" in all the Bible. He is a true example of the Lord's using *"the foolish things to confound the wise."*

Read Judges 6:1 – 7:24

22. What is Israel's situation? _____
_____
_____
_____

23. What was the Lord's command to Gideon (6:14)? _____
_____
_____
_____

24. What was His promise (V. 16)? _____
_____
_____
_____

25. What was the first move Gideon made (v. 25-27)? _____
_____
_____

Once again, we find the enactment of an idea already familiar to us. Before he Lord moves mightily, our idols must be torn down

Finally, after a time of testing the Lord and receiving His reassurance, Gideon was ready to move against the enemy.

26. What was the size of the army approved by the Lord (7:7)?
_____
_____
_____
_____

27. What "weapon" did the army carry (7:16)? _____

_____

_____

28. Describe the battle plan (v. 19-21) _____

_____

_____

_____

_____

29. What was the result of that day? _____

_____

_____

_____

The Old Testament gives us many clear pictures of battles the Lord fought for His people when they followed His military strategy.

Read 2 Kings 18:17-37

This is an account of the Assyrian king Sennacherib's attack on Jerusalem. Following Hezekiah's rebellion against Assyria, Sennacherib sent his army to encompass Jerusalem. The commander of the army tried to persuade the Israelites to surrender, claiming it was impossible for them to withstand him.

30. What is the situation in these verses? _____

_____

_____

_____

Read 2 Kings 19:1-13

31. What was the Lord's assurance to Hezekiah? _____

_____

_____

_____

32. What message did Sennacherib send (v.10)? _____

_____

Read 2 Kings 19:14-37

33. What was the final result? _____

_____

_____

_____

Read 2 Chronicles 14:9-15

34. What is the situation described here? _____

_____

_____

_____

35. How large was their army? _____

_____

_____

_____

36. What was the first thing King Asa did? _____

_____

_____

37. What was the second thing? _____

_____

_____

_____

38. What was the result? _____

_____

_____

_____

When we put our entire faith in the Lord and are obedient to His military strategy, even when we don't understand it and no matter how "foolish" it seems to our natural minds, then the Lord will do battle for us. This is not an easy lesson to learn. Few and far between are the people, both Biblical and of our times, who have lived their lives by it.

A Lack Of Faith

The history of God's people is storied with accounts of people who did not have sufficient faith in God to fight their battles His way.

Read 2 Chronicles 16:1-9

39. What is the situation described here? _____

_____

_____

_____

40. What did Asa do? _____

_____

_____

_____

In his earlier years King Asa had been fervent in His zeal for the Lord, but like so many before and after him, as he grew older, he began to turn to his own devices.

41. What happened militarily? _____

_____

_____

_____

42. What did the Lord say through the prophet? _____

_____

_____

_____

43. What was Asa's reaction? _____

_____

_____

_____

When we are out of the Lord's will, we usually become hostile towards anyone who would remind us of the fact. In this, King Asa was little different from many others.

44. What was the final outcome? _____

_____

Asa had started out his reign boldly. He had torn down the centers of heathen worship and devoted himself to the Lord. How sad it is to see this great king change to a man who, in times of trouble, instead of turning to the Lord, turned to natural ways of making warfare, by forming alliances with heathen nations.

Group Discussion: What do you believe is the spiritual significance of the fact his feet became diseased?

Read 2 Chronicles 34:1- 35:24

45. Briefly summarize the chief events of Josiah's reign. _____
_____
_____
_____

46. Why did King Neco of Egypt come to make war at Carchemish? _____
_____
_____
_____

47. How was Josiah made aware of this? _____
_____
_____
_____

48. What was King Josiah's response? _____
_____
_____
_____

49. With what result? _____
_____
_____
_____

Josiah was another great king, who at first served the Lord whole-heartedly and was greatly blessed for his devotion and obedience. Later when spiritual insight and obedience were needed, he move in the flesh or natural realm.

This is the way of defeat. In the realm of spiritual warfare, we can never depend upon our natural powers of intellect, will and emotions to win battles for us. Rather, we must use the utmost in discernment to distinguish between what the Lord requires of us and what our unruly flesh, in its panic and natural wisdom is urging upon us.

Personal Question: Can you think of some spiritual wars you are trying to fight in the natural at this present time?

Spiritual Disaster

What is it in nature of man that makes him turn away from the Lord, just when God has blessed him abundantly? One sin perhaps more than any other has been and still is the cause of more spiritual disaster than anything else.

Read Numbers 33:52 & 55
50. What commands were the Israelites given when they came into the Promised Land?

_____

_____

_____

_____

Of course, God was talking about actual physical adultery, but "high places" also speak of those areas in our lives where self rather than God is exalted.

As human beings we are particularly subject to the sin of pride. This sin could be called the first sin of the universe, for it was the sin of pride that caused Lucifer's downfall.

Through the history of man, we find this sin occurring again and again, always with devastating results.

Read 2 Chronicles 26: 16-21
Uzziah was a king of Judah who served the Lord well, and the Lord prospered him.

51. What happened to Uzziah after he became strong? _____

_____

_____

_____

52. What was the result? _____

_____

_____

Leprosy is always a type of sin in the Bible. If we allow pride to come into our heart, sin will be the result.

Read 2 Chronicles 32:24-25

Hezekiah was a king of Israel who reinstituted the Passover, restored Temple worship and destroyed the idols in Judah.

53. Yet, at a dark period in his life, what do we learn about Hezekiah?

_____

_____

_____

Read Isaiah 2:11-12

54. What will happen to the proud? _____

_____

_____

_____

Read Proverbs 16:18

55. What does the writer of Proverbs have to say about pride? _____

_____

_____

_____

Read Proverbs 29:23

56. What dos this verse say about a man's pride? _____

_____

_____

_____

Read Isaiah 2:11

57. Who is the only one who will be exalted? _____

_____

Pride, Satan's original sin, is self-exaltation, which is another form of idolatry. It is the old nature's attempt to put itself on the throne and usurp God's glory for self. God has warned that He will share glory with no one.

TO DO:

When you're at home this week, ask God to reveal any unrecognized areas of pride in your life. As He begins to reveal different things, ask His forgiveness and turn these areas over to Him, making sure you "starve" them out by not feeding them with your agreement.

MEMORIZE:

"So he answered, "Do not fear, for those who are with us are more than those who are with them." (2 Kings 6:16)

"For we do not wrestle against flesh and blood, but against principalities, against powers, against the rulers of the darkness of this age, against spiritual hosts of wickedness in the heavenly places." (Ephesians 6:12)

Chapter 8

The Walls

The chief means to defense for ancient Israeli cities were the walls that surrounded them. In fact, throughout much of the Old Testament, the terms city and fortress were synonymous. It is easy to see why. City walls averaged approximately 10 feet in width. At strategic points they could be more than twice that thickness and as high as 30 feet.

Entrance could be gained only through the heavy gates, with its adjacent towers being the most important defense feature in the wall. Special care was taken to increase the strength of the walls at the gateways. If the ordinary thickness of the wall was not considered sufficient, it was doubled there.

These gates were securely locked each day at sundown. Watchmen were employed to watch day and night from the top of the walls to keep an eye out for any sign of enemy activity.

We have already taken note that the Bible compares the Christian to a city on a hill. Just as these ancient cities were protected by their heavy walls, so we have spiritual walls as our main defense against our enemy.

Defense Strategy

Read Isaiah 26:1 and Jeremiah 1:18
1. Who built the walls in these verses? _____

_____

_____

_____

Read Zechariah 2:5
2. Who is the wall in this verse? _____

_____

_____

75

What kind of wall? _____

_____

_____

_____

Read Matthew 21:33

In the parable of the landowner, Jesus described the kind of protection God wants to put around His people.

3. How did the landowner protect His vineyard? _____

_____

_____

_____

Read Isaiah 21:6-8

4. Who are these verses concerned with? _____

_____

_____

_____

5. When is he on duty? _____

_____

_____

_____

Read Ezekiel 33:1-7

6. What is the watchman's duty? _____

_____

_____

_____

Watchmen were not only stationed on the walls to guard against the approach of enemies, but others patrolled the city streets and preserved order.

Read Isaiah 60:18

7. What are the walls called in this verse? _____

_____

_____

_____

The gates? _____

_____

_____

_____

Our salvation is a restraining wall God puts around us to protect us from our enemy, Satan. He even provides watchmen to warn us of the approach of any enemy. If we were able to live in the full aspects of our salvation, our walls would stay intact.

Unfortunately, most of us do not take full advantage of our salvation, and in time sin and Satan make breaches in our wall. If we are not careful to repent and repair the breaches, the damage can become very great.

Breaching The Wall

Let's take a look at some sins that cause holes in our walls.

Read Isaiah 30:12-14

8. What is the Lord's charge against Judah? _____

_____

_____

_____

9. What is their iniquity compared to? _____

_____

_____

_____

Group Discussion: Where is your trust placed? Do you trust in the Lord in such a way that you can rest in Him completely? Do you accept His word as truth or are there sections you have reservations about?

Read Deuteronomy 28:15 & 52

10. What particular sin is the Lord warning of in these verses? _____

_____

_____

_____

11. What did He say would happen if the Israelites did not obey God's commandments?

_____

_____

_____

_____

Moses warned the children of Israel what would happen to them if they did not keep God's statues. In our lives also, we must be obedient to God's commands. Jesus, in the Sermon on the Mount, indicate that the sins of our minds and emotions are as grievous to the Lord as our overt sins.

Personal Application: Is the Holy Spirit convicting you of any sins of disobedience?

Are we bitter and unforgiving? Have we lusted? Have we borne false witness by word or implication? Have we demanded our "rights?" Have we refused those in need? Have we hated our enemies and neglected to pray for them? Have we laid up treasures here on earth? Are we serving mammon? Are we judgmental?

If we have been disobedient in any area of our life, we need to make our confession to the Lord, asking His forgiveness.

Read Numbers 33:52 & 55
12. What commands were the Israelites given when they came into the Promised Land?

_____

_____

_____

_____

Read Isaiah 2:6
13. Why does the Lord say He is rejecting Israel? _____

_____

_____

_____

Of all the abominations the Israelites committed, idolatry was the one the Lord absolutely refused to tolerate.

Group Discussion: Why do you think God hates idolatry so much?

When anyone practices idolatry, he is worshipping another god. God will not tolerate this. Time and time again, as His people turned from Him to worship other gods, He punished them, eventually giving them over in captivity to the most idolatrous nation of all, Babylon. When the Israelites finally returned from Babylon, idolatry had been completely removed from them.

Nowhere else is "idol worship" more disastrous than in the area of spiritual warfare. When we have idols (other gods of ambition, material gods, other people, anything that stands between us and God) in our life, then we are in effect, trying to serve two commanders, Jesus and Satan.

Personal Question: Identify any idols you may have in your life. Are you ready to give them up? Take time right now to tell Jesus, then do whatever He tells you to do.

We have looked at some ways the walls of protection God has put around us can be breached or even torn down. We have done all we are able to make ourselves right with God. However, before we are ready to repair and rebuild our walls, there is one more step to take.

Building The Temple

Many years before the Prophet Nehemiah returned to Jerusalem to rebuild the walls of that holy city, an important event preceded him.

Read Ezra 1:1-3
14. What had God commanded the king of Persia to do? _____
_____
_____
_____

15. Was this accomplished? _____
_____
_____
_____

Read 1 Corinthians 3:16

16. What is the temple of God today? _____

_____

_____

17. Who dwells there? _____

_____

_____

Read Romans 12:1
18. What does Paul tell us to do with our bodies? _____

_____

_____

Read 1 Thessalonians 4:4
19. What does Paul tell us to do with our vessels (bodies)? _____

_____

_____

God has chosen the hearts and bodies of believers as His temple and His dwelling place rather than any man-made structure. Possessing them in sanctification and honor is a prerequisite to any rebuilding that is done.

Group Discussion: Do you have the confidence and peace that come from having given not only your heart, but your body as well to God as a holy sacrifice? Are you caring for your body in a way that allows Satan no entrance?

Finally, we are ready to look at the process that goes on in the rebuilding and restoring of God's walls around the believer.

Restoring Our Walls

During the Diaspora, the scattering of the Jews, Nehemiah was the royal cupbearer to King Artaxerxes of Persia.

Read Nehemiah 1

20. What news did Nehemiah receive about Jerusalem? _____

_____

_____

_____

_____

_____

_____

_____

21. Summarize his prayer. _____

_____

_____

_____

_____

_____

22. How does he identify Israel's sins in verse 6-7? _____

_____

_____

_____

Read Nehemiah 2:1-9

23. What was Nehemiah's request of the king? _____

_____

_____

_____

24. How did the king respond? _____

_____

_____

_____

Nehemiah was successful in his plea to the king and received permission to return to Jerusalem to rebuild the wall. He also provided him with the necessary credentials and the means of obtaining supplies.

Read Nehemiah 2:11-18
Nehemiah did not tell anyone in Jerusalem his plans until after he had inspected the situation.

25. What did he finally tell them (v.17)? _____

_____

_____

_____

_____

26. What was their response? _____

_____

_____

Many can identify with the condition of Jerusalem. For one reason or another, through our own fault or ignorance, Satan has devastated our lives. Our walls of protection have been torn down, our gates burned with fire. Our condition is a reproach to God's work in us.

If we only have the eyes to see and the ears to hear, we can hear God telling us, "Come, let us rebuild." Let our response be as was that of the people to who Nehemiah spoke, "Let us arise and build."

Read Nehemiah 3:1
27. What was built first? _____

_____

_____

_____

Group Discussion: Do you remember what the gates were called in Isaiah 60:18? What relationship do you see between praise and the "gates" of your wall of protection?

When we make a habit of praising the Lord, it's difficult for Satan to find an entrance into our lives.

Read Nehemiah 3:12

28. Who is mentioned in this verse? _____

_____

_____

Being a woman doesn't disqualify you from this important work of the Lord. Whenever we do the Lord's work in restoring or rebuilding, we can expect trouble from the enemy. The following verses are a record of much of the building and tactics of the enemies of the builders.

Enemy Strategy

Read Nehemiah 4:1-3

29. What did Sanballat and Tobiah feel and say about the work of rebuilding?

_____

_____

_____

_____

The background of these two men is interesting, Sanballat, the apparent ringleader, whose name means, "The moon god, Sin, has given life," was an influential Samaritan. His partner, Tobiah was a member of a family, whose members came back to Jerusalem after the captivity, but failed to prove their descent.

Read Nehemiah 4:4-6

30. What was Nehemiah's response to their ridicule and mocking? _____

_____

_____

_____

31. What effect did their ridicule have on the workers?

_____

_____

_____

Whenever we are involved in God's work, we can expect trouble from God's enemies.

Nehemiah, however, knew how to turn an attack into a triumph. Rather than overly seeking revenge, he turned to the Lord, and God brought good out of the situation.

Read Nehemiah 4:7-8

32. What was the enemy's next plan of attack? _____

_____

_____

_____

33. How did Nehemiah combat this latest threat? _____

_____

_____

_____

How wise Nehemiah was. Although he took precautions in the natural, his real trust was in the Lord.

34. What was the result as far as the enemies were concerned? _____

_____

_____

_____

35. What was the result as far as Nehemiah's people were concerned?

_____

_____

_____

Read Nehemiah 4:16-19 & 23

36. How was the work performed after this? _____

_____

_____

_____

_____

Read Nehemiah 5:1-5

37. What was the next problem? _____

_____

_____

_____

38. What did Nehemiah do? _____

39. What was the result of the meeting? _____

_____

_____

_____

Read Nehemiah 6:1-9

40. What did Nehemiah enemies do next? _____

_____

_____

_____

41. What was his response? _____

_____

_____

_____

42. What was their next step? _____

_____

_____

_____

43. What was Nehemiah's response? _____

_____

_____

_____

Read Nehemiah 6:10-16

44. What was the next step of the enemy? _____

_____

_____

_____

45. How did Nehemiah respond? _____

46. What did he perceive about Shemaiah? _____

_____

_____

47. When was the wall finished? _____

_____

_____

48. What was the effect on their enemies? _____

_____

_____

We cannot expect Satan to give up his attacks until the very last moment, but in the end, when we have rebuilt and completely restored God's protective walls, he is forced to admit defeat.

TO DO:

Before new strong walls can be rebuilt, we must clear out the rubble. Ask God to reveal the rubble of idolatry in your heart. This can be anything that you have placed above God in your life – material goods, social media, friends, your family, food, etc. Deal with these areas as God directs you.

MEMORIZE:

"Violence shall no longer be heard in your land, neither wasting nor destruction within your borders; But you shall call your walls salvation, and your gates praise." (Isaiah 60:18)

Chapter 9

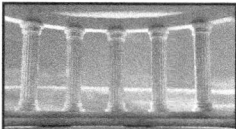

The Fifth Column

During the Spanish Civil War, supporters of the rebel forces formed a clandestine, subversive organization which worked in Madrid, the enemy territory, to help their own political and military cause. One rebel general who was leading four columns of troops against the city, named the subversive group "The Fifth Column." Today this term remains a picturesque addition to our vocabulary, meaning an enemy working secretly from within.

Would you be surprised to learn that we also have a "fifth column" within our own walls – a fifth column that is more than ready to cooperate with Satan? We have heard it described by several names – our inner being, our core or center, the essence of what we are. In Scripture it is referred to frequently as the flesh.

Armed Struggle

Read Ephesians 2:8-9

1. What does Paul tell us about our salvation? _____
_____
_____
_____

2. What is it not? _____
_____
_____
_____

3. Why did God make it entirely a gift? _____
_____
_____
_____

Read Romans 7:18

4 What does Paul tell us about the flesh? _____

_____

_____

_____

When Paul tells us that nothing good dwells in our flesh that is exactly what he means. That is God's judgment of the flesh. As humans we like to believe that we really aren't so bad. Maybe we get off the track now and then, but human nature is basically good – basically worth redeeming – worth saving.

The Bible teaches just the opposite. In fact, in Romans 5:10 Paul says that before salvation, man is God's enemy and needs to be reconciled to God through Christ. God did not save us because we were worth saving, but because of His great love for us.

Group Discussion: Are you ready to accept God's verdict on our basic nature? How do you feel about the idea that none of us has anything in us that is worth saving?

The Bible, both Old and New Testaments, has much to say on the subject of man's inherent evil.

Read Jeremiah 17:9

5. What does this passage tell us about our "heart?" _____

_____

_____

_____

The heart is just another term for our inner man.

When Jesus began His teaching ministry on earth, He echoed the words of the prophet.

Read Matthew 15:19-20

6. What does Jesus say comes out of the heart? _____

_____

_____

_____

7. What do these things do to us? _____

_____

_____

_____

8. Look up the word "defile" in a dictionary and paraphrase the definition.

_____

_____

_____

_____

If a man were not born defiled as a result of the Fall, he would ultimately become defiled by his own thought process and deeds.

Paul in the Book of Romans amplifies this same thought.

Read Romans 1:18-32

9. Why does Paul say anyone who does not believe in God has no excuse?

_____

_____

_____

10. In what way? _____

_____

_____

_____

_____

11. What has lack of honoring God done? _____

_____

_____

_____

Paul is not implying that this happens in exactly the same way to each individual who does not honor God, but we can safely say this is an accurate picture of what happens to societies as a whole that do not honor Him, and eventually it happens to all individuals in that society.

Group Discussion: Using Paul's list as a comparison, what happens to our own country since we as a nation have stopped honoring God? What happens to people when God enters their life and they are saved?

At War With The Spirit

At salvation God gives us His Holy Spirit. We might think that with God's Spirit in man, all hostility to God would end. However that is not the case.

Read Galatians 5:17
12. What does this verse tell us about the relationship between the flesh and the Spirit?

_____

_____

_____

_____

One big area of spiritual warfare is the battle that goes on between our flesh and the Holy Spirit of God within us. It is a battle that will go on to some degree throughout our lifetime.

Read Galatians 5:19-21
13. What are the deeds of the flesh? _____

_____

_____

_____

14. Who is Paul talking to in his letter? _____

_____

_____

Did you think these were the characteristics of the unsaved? NO, Paul is talking to Christians.

Group Discussion: Do any of the things on this list surprise you?

No one can deny the complete wickedness of Satan, but it does us no good to accuse him of being responsible for things that are the works of our own flesh. Let's look at another area for which many mistakenly blame Satan.

More Hostilities

Read James 1:14

15. How are we tempted? _____

_____

_____

_____

_____

Although the meaning of the word "lust" has changed, the Greek word from which it is translated simply means a desire which can either be good or bad. The form of the word used here has a prefix which intensifies its meaning. In this case, it is not only a desire, but a craving.

Perhaps you have been taught that temptation was entirely the work of the devil. True, he is the tempter, but in this verse, James explains that it is our own lusts –our own evil desires for things that cause us to respond to the temptation.

Personal Question: Is there some temptation in your life that you have been wrongly blaming Satan for? If so, you need to be willing to concede that it is a product of our own desire.

16. What happens to our "lusts" when we don't deal with them? _____

_____

_____

_____

_____

Unsaved man stands in a complete hopeless situation, as far as his own nature, his own abilities and his own worth, but even saved man quickly becomes aware that he cannot be "good" by his own efforts. The war is not over. Even though we have the Holy Spirit residing within us, there is still something in us that makes us want to oppose Him and continue to desire things that are not eternal. Like Paul, we want to cry out to be saved from this certainty of sin, corruption and death. It is part of the Good News that God has provided a way out.

Read Ezekiel 11:19

17. What was God's promise to Israel? _____

_____

_____

God was promising that the day would come when He would take that old dead heart, that sinful center of man, and replace it with a living heart.

18. What would this new heart do? _____

_____

_____

_____

Read Jeremiah 31:33

19. What would be different about God's New Covenant? _____

_____

_____

_____

God was looking forward to a day when His people would no longer be just external followers of His laws. He was looking forward to a time when their heart would desire to follow after Him.

Read Galatians 4:4

20. When did this happen? _____

_____

_____

_____

Read Romans 7:25

21. What does Jesus do for us when He saves us? _____

_____

_____

_____

Group Discussion: If this is true, why don't we always experience it?

We don't always experience it because we don't always cooperate with the Spirit of God within us. According to the Bible, every Christian – a man, woman and child has a new heart provided by God Himself, a heart that wants to be obedient to God. We have the Spirit of God resident in us, a Spirit that moment by moment urges us toward a fuller, more complete realization of the new nature God has given us. This process is called "sanctification." In order to fully realize this new nature, we must cooperate with the Holy Spirit. Let's look at some ways we can do this.

Present Yourself To God

Read Romans 6:12-14
22. How do we let sin reign in our bodies? _____

_____

_____

_____

23. What should we do instead? _____

_____

_____

_____

Read Romans 12:1-2
24. What else should we do with our bodies? _____

_____

_____

_____

We remember that the Old Testament sacrifice was the dead body of an animal. Under the New Covenant, the acceptable sacrifice becomes the living body of the believer.

Read Ephesians 4:22
25. What should we do? _____

_____

_____

_____

Group Discussion: How do we lay aside the old self? Does Romans 6:11 help?

We lay aside our old self by giving it no credence, no recognition. We reject its demands and refuse to gratify its lusts.

Some Good News

Read Colossians 3:10

26. With what do you replace the old self? _____

_____

_____

Read Ephesians 4:24

27. Describe the new self. _____

_____

_____

_____

_____

_____

Read 2 Peter 1:2-10

28. What has God granted us? _____

_____

_____

_____

Group Discussion: Are you willing to believe this with no reservations that God has granted us everything we will ever need for life and godliness? If not, why not?

29. How is this granted? _____

_____

_____

_____

Group Discussion: How do we gain true knowledge of God?

True knowledge of God is gained through reading and studying the Bible and being obedient to what it teaches, by praying and meditating, by praising and worshipping God, and by fellowshipping with other believers. Gaining true knowledge of God then becomes an important weapon in our war against Satan and his lies.

30. Why has God given us His wonderful promises? _____

31. What should we do for this reason? _____

_____

_____

_____

32. If we practice these things what can we be certain of? _____

_____

_____

_____

Refitting Time

Read Colossians 3:10-11

33. What is happening to this new self? _____

_____

_____

_____

Here we are back to the importance of the true knowledge of God.

34. What kind of a renewal is it? _____

_____

_____

_____

In his epistle, James speaks to this same idea.

Read James 2:1-13

35. What attitude does James condemn? _____

_____

_____

_____

36. What does he say we are doing when we show partiality (v.9)?

37. What should we be doing (v.8)? _____

_____

_____

_____

38. What are we guilty of when we don't? _____

_____

_____

_____

Personal Question: Have you been guilty of this sin? If so, what do you need to do?

Read Ephesians 4:23
39. Specifically, where are we renewed? _____

_____

_____

Read Romans 12:2
40. Why should we be renewed in our minds? _____

_____

_____

41. What does this renewing of the mind replace? _____

_____

_____

_____

Read 1 John 2:15-16
42. What is our attitude toward the world supposed to be? _____

_____

_____

_____

Read 1 Timothy 6:10

43. What is one thing in the world we are specifically told not to love?

_____

_____

_____

44. What is the love of money? _____

_____

_____

_____

45. What has it caused? _____

_____

_____

_____

Some have called materialism the sin of our culture. Each of us needs to ask the Holy Spirit to search our heart and tell us whether or not we are guilty of this sin.

Read Galatians 5:16

46. How can we keep from carrying out the desires of the flesh? _____

_____

_____

_____

Read 1 Timothy 6:11

47. What are we to pursue? _____

_____

_____

_____

Read Hebrews 12:1-2

48. With what does Paul compare the Christian walk? _____

_____

_____

_____

49. Who are our eyes to be fixed on? _____

_____

_____

_____

Keeping our eyes on Satan, our problems or our sins, WILL ALWAYS lead us to a dead end. Rather, as we walk in the Spirit, we must keep our eyes on our Commander in Chief, to see His instructions for us are.

TO DO:

It's not easy to accept the fact that the enemy is of our own flesh. Determine ways you may have been cooperating with Satan and his schemes. Then take authority over the areas where you should have self-control and ask Jesus to strengthen you in your resolve.

MEMORIZE:

"But this is the covenant that I will make with the house of Israel after those days, says the Lord: I will put My law in their minds, and write it on their hearts; and I will be their God, and they shall be My people." (Jeremiah 31:33)

"...and have put on the new man who is renewed in knowledge according to the image of Him who created him..." (Colossians 3:10)

Chapter 10

The Lord's Warrior

The Good Soldier

Read 2 Timothy 2:4

1. In the first chapter we considered what a good soldier does. Now we need to look at what he does not do. What is that? _____

_____

_____

_____

The word entangled has the implication of becoming entwined in something from which it is difficult to free ourselves, such as a net or snare.

Group Discussion: What, if any activities are you involved with to the point of entanglement?

Read Deuteronomy 20:5-7

God has always taken into account that not everyone, for one reason or another, makes a good soldier.

2. In the laws of warfare given to the children of Israel, who was excluded from the fighting? _____

_____

_____

_____

Group Discussion: Why do you think these people in particular were exempt from the army?

These were all people who had other major interests in life, therefore, it is doubtful whether or not they would make good soldiers.

Group Discussion: Is Paul saying we are not to become involved in anything that is not the

Lords work?

While we might have to be involved in some secular activities, we should not become involved in them to the extent that we cannot easily extricate ourselves. Our chief aim in life must always be to please the One who enlisted us.

No Room For Cowards

Read Deuteronomy 20:8
3. Who is exempt in this verse? _____

_____

_____

_____

Read Judges 7:1-6
4. In the formation of Gideon's army, who was sent away? _____

_____

_____

_____

Warfare, spiritual or otherwise has no room for cowards. We who have the authority of the Lord Jesus and faith in the fact that "the battle is the Lord's" need not fear Satan and his cohorts.

Group Discussion: If the Lord had His trumpeter sound the battle cry right now, would you be there in the front ranks or would you have to put in for an exemption?

The Bible tells us we are priests, prophets and kings. We're going to see how these three roles relate to spiritual warfare.

Priests

After God had led the Israelites out of Egypt, He established Aaron, Moses' older brother and his sons as priests to minister to Him. Later, He called the entire Tribe of the Levites, rather than the first-born sons of all tribes to be a priesthood.

What was the priests' part in warfare? Let's look at three important episodes in Scripture.

In The Front Ranks

Read Joshua 3:14-17

5. In the account of the children of Israel's crossing of the Jordan, where are the priests positioned? _____

_____

_____

6. What did they carry? _____

_____

The Ark of the Covenant was the "dwelling place" of the Lord. By marching out ahead of the entire camp, holding the Ark of the Covenant high, the priests enabled the people to keep their eyes on and their confidence in the Lord.

7. What happened when the priests stepped into the river? _____

_____

_____

_____

8. Where did the priests wait? _____

_____

_____

_____

Read Joshua 4:1-18

9. What happened before they were allowed to cross over to the other side?

_____

_____

_____

10. What happened when the priests left the water? _____

_____

_____

_____

Read Joshua 6:1-21

11. In the account of the capture of Jericho, how were the people arranged as they marched around Jericho? _____

_____

_____

_____

12. What were the instructions given? _____

_____

` _____

Read 2 Chronicles 20:21-25

You will remember from your previous reading of this section on King Jehoshaphat, that Judah was about to be attacked by heathen nations. The previous day the Lord had promised victory. Now the day of the battle dawned.

13. Who did Jehoshaphat appoint? _____

_____

_____

_____

14. What was their position in the fighting? _____

_____

_____

_____

15. What happen? _____

_____

_____

_____

No spiritual coward can ever function effectively as a priest. In all spiritual warfare the priests are in the front ranks, if not actually moving before the others, then following right behind the leaders. What does this say to us?

We have looked at singing, praise and worship as spiritual weapons, but now we want to look at another aspect of what the priestly ministry represents.

Read 2 Chronicles 20:21

16. How were the priests attired? _____

_____

_____

_____

Glance through Leviticus 11:1-46

17. What are these verses concerned with? _____

_____

_____

_____

18. What is the priest's relationship to anything unclean? _____

_____

_____

_____

(We find much of Leviticus concerned with the avoidance of anything unclean)
The priesthood and its duties speak of separation from sin, and of holiness. We find
very stringent demands being placed upon the priesthood in every area of their life.

Read Leviticus 21 and 22

19. What was the regulation concerning dead bodies? _____

_____

_____

_____

20. What was the regulation concerning marriage? _____

_____

_____

_____

21. What was the regulation concerning defects? _____

_____

_____

_____

22. What was the regulation concerning the holy gifts? _____

_____

_____

_____

(We also find numerous occasions of additional cleansing)

Read Numbers 8:6-7

23. How were the Levites cleanse? _____

_____

_____

_____

Read Deuteronomy 23:9-14

24. What duty of the priests is described here? _____

_____

_____

_____

_____

Read Joshua 3:5

25. What was Joshua's command to the Israelites the night before they crossed the Jordan? _____

_____

_____

26. What would happen the next day? _____

_____

_____

_____

Read Joshua 5:1-8

27. What did the Lord tell Joshua to do after the Israelites crossed the Jordan?

_____

_____

_____

28. Why was this necessary? _____

_____

Immediately following the Israelites' spectacular crossing of the Jordan River, the Israelites were encamped in the very face of their enemies. At this point the Lord demanded that they be circumcised, an operation that would make them entirely vulnerable should the enemy attack.

29. How did the Lord protect them (v.1)? _____

_____

_____

Consecration, cleansing and circumcision also speak of holiness. In the Old Testament, cleansing and holiness were largely concerned with external deeds – in the New Testament sanctification is an internal process. Before the Lord will go with us into battle, He makes sure we are clothed in His righteousness and that we are clean, even when the cleansing process puts us in a disadvantage position in the natural. If we would see the Lord do wonders among us, we must be certain our hearts and lives are clean.

A Holy Camp

Read Deuteronomy 23:9
30. What does this verse tell us about warfare? _____

_____

_____

Anyone who enters spiritual combat with known sin in their life is foolish. The Book of Joshua relates one instance in which the commission of a sin had disastrous results upon the entire army.

Read Joshua 7:1-5
31. What do these verses describe? _____

_____

_____

Read Joshua 7:10-13

32. When Joshua went before the Lord, what did the Lord reveal to him?

_____

_____

_____

33. What had been done specifically? _____

_____

_____

_____

34. What would happen to the Israelites as far as battle was concerned?

_____

_____

_____

This incident took place shortly after the Israelites' spectacular victory over Jericho. In the natural it would seem that God had picked a very poor time to chasten His people – just when the heathen nations were paralyzed with fear at the very thought of the Israelites. But God's first priority is always to deal with the sin in our lives.

Read Joshua 7:14-24

35. Who was the guilty party? _____

_____

_____

_____

36. What was done? _____

_____

_____

_____

The uncleanness was swept from the camp, and immediately afterward, the Israelites defeated Ai.

Read 1 Peter 2:9

37. What does Peter tell us about ourselves in this verse? _____

_____

38. For what purpose? _____

_____

_____

_____

Read 1 Peter 2:5

39. What is the duty of the priests given here? _____

_____

_____

In the Old Testament, one of the prime duties of the priests was to offer up physical sacrifices, the bodies of bulls, sheep and goats.

God is commanding today another kind of sacrifice – spiritual sacrifices from His priests.

Read Psalm 51:17

40. What sacrifices are mentioned here? _____

_____

_____

The Bible speaks of many sacrifices we can make to the Lord as part of our priestly duties – the sacrifice of righteousness, the sacrifice of thanksgiving, and a sacrifice of praise.

Group Discussion: Do you make sacrifices to God on a daily basis?

Prophets

Read Hosea 9:8

42. What does the Lord call Ephraim, other than prophet? _____

_____

_____

_____

Read Ezekiel 33:1-9

43. What is the watchman's duty? _____

_____

_____

_____

44. What happens to the watchman who does not warn? _____

_____

_____

This is undoubtedly the idea Paul was referring to in Acts 18:6 when he cried to the resisting Jews in Corinth, ***"Your blood be on your heads I am clean."***

Read Ezekiel 3:17

45. What was the Lord's command to the prophet Jeremiah? _____

_____

_____

_____

Group Discussion: Have we neglected this part of our ministry as the Lord's warriors? Have we adequately warned the world and even God's people of the great danger that encompasses and threatens to overtake? Have we spoken God's Word to them?

Read 1 Thessalonians 5:1-10

This same idea of watching and being on the alert is given in the New Testament.

46. What are we to be on the alert about? _____

_____

_____

_____

Read Isaiah 62:6-7

47. What does God command the watchman to do? _____

_____

_____

_____

We usually associate the ministry of intercession with the priests, but here God clearly calls His watchmen to "remind" Him of what He has promised to do for Jerusalem.

Personal Question: Have you been a faithful watchman and made intercession to God, reminding him of His great and wonderful promises for His Church?

Kings

Read 1 Peter 2:9

48. What kind of priesthood are we? _____

_____

_____

_____

Royalty implies the role of a king. Let's look at the function of kings in warfare.

Read 2 Samuel 11:1

49. What time of the year was it? _____

_____

_____

_____

Kings usually went to battle in the spring when food was plentiful. The armies of those days lived off the land.

Read 1 Samuel 8:19-20

This is the passage in which the Israelites demand that Samuel give them a king. Samuel had just related to them all the disadvantages having a king would entail, but they would not be dissuaded.

50. Some of their reasons for wanting a king were that they might be like the other nations, that their king might judge them and _____

_____

_____

_____

Read 1 Samuel 13:3-4

Shortly after Saul was chosen king, trouble with the Philistines broke out.

51. What did Saul do? _____

_____

_____

_____

Group Discussion: What does the king represent to you?

We hope you answered authority and power. A king represents the nation, the people he rules over. He alone has certain authority and power.

Read 1 Samuel 16:1-13

Following the Lord's rejection of King Saul as king because of his disobedience, He sent Samuel to Jesse's house.

52. What was Samuel's purpose for being there? _____

_____

_____

_____

53. Why did Samuel anoint him? _____

_____

_____

Read 1 Samuel 17:50

54. What does his verse describe? _____

_____

_____

_____

55. Did this happen before or after his anointing as king? _____

_____

_____

_____

In other words David had already been anointed king before he defeated Goliath. Even though the people did not recognize it at the time, they had been spared from the Philistines by the victory of their true king.

Christians are in much the same position as David was. Although we do not look like kings and few think of us as kings, in Gods eyes we are already kings.

As spiritual kings, we need to accept our authority in the Lord and lead the less brave in our spiritual warfare against our enemy.

Before a king went off to battle, sacrifices were made. Psalm 20 is believed to be a liturgical (public) prayer which accompanied this sacrifice.

Read Psalm 20

56. What form of prayer are the first five verses? _____

_____

_____

_____

57. What is the rest of the psalm concerned with? _____

_____

_____

_____

58. Who will the psalmist boast in? _____

_____

_____

Priests, prophet and king – ALL ARE WARRIORS IN THE LORD'S ARMY.

TO DO:

Think and pray over what you have learned. How can you apply it in your spiritual warfare?

MEMORIZE:

"You also, as living stones, are being built up a spiritual house, a holy priesthood, to offer up spiritual sacrifices acceptable to God through Jesus Christ."
(1 Peter 2:5)

Chapter 11

Nothing Less Than Total Victory!

One of the problems in spiritual warfare is that too many times we stop fighting long before the battle is over. We claim victory as soon as we win a small skirmish or force the enemy to give a little ground. This incomplete victory is very different from the warfare God commanded the children of Israel to make as they took over the Promised Land.

Discussion Question: How do we know when to stop fighting?

Unconditional Surrender

Read Exodus 23:20-23
1. What was God's command to the Israelites? _____

_____

_____

_____

2. If they were obedient, what did God promise to be to them?

_____

_____

_____

3. What did He promise to do for them? _____

_____

_____

_____

Notice that the requirement for God's destruction of the enemy was their complete obedience.

Read Deuteronomy 20:13-16
4. God made a distinction between two kinds of cities and how they were to be treated.

112

What was the distinction based on? _____

_____

_____

_____

God's Terms

Read Exodus 23:23-30

5. What were the Israelites forbidden to do? _____

_____

_____

_____

6. What were they commanded to do? _____

_____

_____

_____

7. What personal blessings did the Lord promise the Israelites for their obedience?

_____

_____

_____

8. What did He promise to do militarily? _____

_____

_____

_____

Group Discussion: What is the implication of their enemies turning their backs on them?

9. Summarize how God was going to do this? _____

_____

_____

_____

God gave very practical orders to the Israelites. Understanding their human limitations, He planned the capture of the Promised Land to be on a gradual basis.

Read Exodus 34:10-17 and Deuteronomy 7:15

10. What further obedience was required by God? _____

_____

_____

11. What was God's very practical reason for these commands (Ex. 34:12)?

_____

_____

_____

Read Numbers 21:1-3

12. What vow did the Israelites make with God? _____

_____

_____

_____

Read Numbers 21:33-35

13. What did they do to the king of Basham? _____

_____

_____

_____

14. Read the following Scriptures, then write what the Israelites did to the enemy in each case.

Numbers 31:10-11 _____

_____

Joshua 6:21 _____

_____

Joshua 8:24-27 _____

_____

Joshua 10:31-32 _____

_____

Joshua 10:34-35 _____

_____

Joshua 10:38-39 _____

_____

Joshua 10:40 _____

_____

Joshua 11:8-9 _____

_____

Joshua 11:11-12 _____

_____

Joshua 11:19-20 _____

_____

Judges 1:17 _____

_____

I think we're beginning to get the point. In each case the Israelites were to fight until the enemy was completely destroyed.

If we are repelled by all this bloodshed and find it hard to accept the fact that God would command His people to be so blood-thirsty, we need to remind ourselves of two import ant facts. First, these were heathen people whom God knew would turn His people away from Him if they were allowed tc live side by side with the Israelites.

Secondly, we need to remember that the accounts of the wars of the Old Testament, which were fought in the natural, are there to provide us with a picture of what we Christians are supposed to do in the Spirit. God made some fantastic promises to the Israelites if they would only be obedient to Him in this matter.

Read Leviticus 26:3-8
15. Summarize the promises God made to the Israelites. _____

_____

_____

_____

_____

_____

_____

_____

Sadly, the history of Israel is not one of obedience. Everything God had warned the children of Israel would happen if they were less than totally obedient to Him did, in fact, happen.

Read Judges 1:28
16. What had God said would happen? _____

_____

_____

Read Judges 2:11-15
18. What eventually happened? _____

_____

_____

19. How did God punish them? _____

_____

_____

How does all this apply to the spiritual warfare Christians are supposed to wage? It applies in this way – when we engage our enemy in battle, we must be determined and have the endurance to fight through to complete victory.

But how do we know when the battle is completely over? Obviously, in any kind of spiritual warfare, we have to strongly rely on spiritual discernment, but there are two lessons we can learn from the Old Testament warfare that are missing factors in so much of the warfare we conduct today. The first is the use of our time during period of peace.

Keeping The Peace

Read 2 Chronicles 14:2-7

20. How is Asa described in verse 2? _____

_____

_____

_____

21. What is the last sentence in verse 5? _____

_____

_____

_____

22. What did he do during this time? _____

_____

_____

_____

We might expect that as warriors, we would be allowed some time off between battles. But we see that during these times of rest, we must fortify ourselves in the Lord.

Group Discussion: How can we, as Christian soldiers, fortify ourselves in the Lord?

To The Victors

A look at several passages of Scripture will show us our second failure.

Read Numbers 31:10-11

23. What did the Israelites do following their victory? _____

_____

_____

_____

24. Read the following Scriptures and list the results of victory in each case.

Joshua 11:14 _____

_____

2 Chronicles 17:10-13 _____

_____

2 Chronicles 20:25 _____

_____

Numbers 31:32-35 _____

_____

Those engaged in spiritual warfare should be seeing tremendous victories. We should not only be winning the individual battles we set out to accomplish, but we should be reaping spiritual dividends as well.

Read 2 Chronicles 14:9-14
Later in the reign of King Asa, Judah was attacked by Zerah, the Ethiopian.

25. Who did King Asa turn to for help? _____

_____

_____

_____

26. Why was King Asa able to destroy all the cities around Gerar?

_____

_____

_____

Whenever the Lord's people stood up as strong men, we see this same pattern repeated.

Read Joshua 2:8-11
27. In this account of Rahab and the Israeli spies, what does Rahab tell the two men?

_____

_____

_____

The exploits of God's mighty warriors have the power to strike terror into the hearts of Satan's troops. We should never be satisfied with small victories – we should keep up the warfare until the enemy turn's tail and runs, leaving behind the spoils of lives set free. Whole areas coming out from under the dominion of the wicked one.

Read Luke 4:18-19

We have been given our objective and our marching orders.

28. What did Jesus say He had come to do? _____

_____

_____

_____

How many prisoners have you released lately? How many in bondage have you set free? If this was Jesus' job while He was on earth, isn't it even more so our job now that He has returned to heaven and left the establishing of the Kingdom in our hands?

Group Discussion: Can you share a time when you successfully fought a spiritual battle? What were the spoils? Share the details. _____

_____

_____

_____

_____

_____

Read Luke 11:17-22

29. Who is the strong man of this passage? _____

_____

_____

_____

30. What was his previous position? _____

_____

_____

_____

31. Who is the One stronger? _____

_____

_____

_____

32. What has He done to the strong man? _____

_____

_____

_____

This is a picture of how Jesus described Himself, even before Calvary. Think of how much more power He has over Satan today.

Group Discussion: If Jesus has given us His authority, what does that make us today in terms of the parable told by Jesus?

YES, Jesus has left us fully armed, with the power to destroy the strong man who is illegally living in the territory that rightfully belongs to Jesus and to us. It is time we began our warfare in earnest, settling for nothing less than total victory.

Ministry Information

Hosanna World Changers is a church with a God-given vision to reach the lost, disciple those who are being saved, and release God's servants [those being equipped] into the work of ministy. It is our desire to reach both the lost in our community and around the world. For more information regarding our ministry, please email us at:

tcarubba@hosannawc.com

Or call our offices at:

(956) 831-5750

Our ministry & church are located at:

Hosanna World Changers
2400 Dr. Hugh Emerson Rd.
Brownsville, Texas 78526

NOTES

NOTES

NOTES

NOTES

NOTES

NOTES

NOTES

NOTES

NOTES

NOTES